One momei

Al;o by David Bunn and published by Ginninderra Press
The Great Scheme

David Bunn

One moment human

In memory of
Mercia Josephine Bunn (26 February 1919–14 July 2005)
and
Clifford George Bunn (2 March 1915–28 May 1997)

One moment human
ISBN 978 1 76109 502 3
Copyright © text David Bunn 2023
Cover image: *Elantxobe*, David Bunn, 2015

First published 2023 by
GINNINDERRA PRESS
PO Box 3461 Port Adelaide 5015
www.ginninderrapress.com.au

Contents

In my country

Progress of the soul

A hint of echo mocks us from the wings.
A songbird's incognito in the choir –
one moment human, gone the next.

Elantxobe

I – Poco a Poco!

a woman mutters on the path above,
waving a fistful of plucked herbs,
against my rush up from the port

which you, unkind wife, dared me to –
chase you up breakneck crumbling cliffs,
below the landslide netting, scramble
the last gasping flight to our square

where the grandmothers perch at dusk,
plump birds on their village bench,
and shout in their aprons like they've time
to burn, like something new happened,
just now, and must be told and retold,
gathering vehemence with each recount,

as though the tide is not about to turn.

II – One oar

Flung on the deck, worn grey churning green water,
blue as the Virgin's mantle till salt tore the pigment from you,

you are cracked and destitute and twine rebinds you,
but your double lies off in a boat shed.

A lifetime working a quiet harbour, and this is what happens –
salt-flayed and failing, but somewhere an unsullied self abides.

III – A problem with green

'Green' will not serve for this misted harbour
when the tide is in and the water billows

like a flung sheet falling to a bed
like dark glass dimpled as it cools.

The harbour glowers deeper than polished stone,
a chunk of liquid emerald, big as a football field.

Someone hammered pewter over magma,
or it's the hue of cloud-saddened conifers.

IV – A battered red-decked dinghy

Behind the sea wall she hovers on glass darkness.
Braided coils of light loop navy-green around her.

Salt spray, sun and gales, the fret of mooring lines,
have scoured her deck to a mottle of dulled rose.

She stirs, she skates on living water. Swerves
her battered bow towards the entrance.

She'll skip port on the turning of the tide;
and then come the big blows.

The progress of the soul

Once when I was king in Babylon
I withered for lack of dreams
but could not sleep for fear of them.

One dream – a thousand open graves.
My prophet smiled a crooked smile
– Behold your feet of clay.

Suddenly, if I try speech, I yawp,
a once happy swine suddenly possessed
by a devil howling for its paradise.

Like a deer that pants in the psalms
I thirsted for a drink I never found:
luscious as peach, as lucid as white wine.

A plucked guitar echoes in the boughs,
laments delights I have never known,
but I am devastated by their loss.

A moth beats at a darkened pane,
at a flicker of reflection,
battering for a brilliance beyond.

Solomon sings of perfumed breasts
gleaming in his chamber, but priests say
it is for his God the king yearns.

Concert at Köln 1975

I

The foyer chimes have rung their summoning tune
and he begins with that, which then he turns
into a melody you know, or used to know –

as though standards flutter in the German air
ready to be gathered in his net of strings –
and all those songs, somehow, once were yours.

I wait expectant, after forty years, for when
he sweeps arpeggios downwise, on and on,
each layered on the others, loud pedal down,

surround him with harmonic flittering ghosts,
faintest sounds, you can't be certain that you heard,
shimmering in deep chaos of the chords.

As though you stand on a northern beach
and tilt your mind to the aurora's sidelong lights,
to squeeze some meaning from the writhe and swirl

above the racing surfaces of seas and clouds.
Which I never did – somehow I missed the chance –
and I'm never going to get to Iceland now.

II

My father was bronze idol or black box –
I could never tell what was happening inside,
and then sudden he'd pronounce for certain:

You read the next page while your fingers play
this one, he tells me, about playing from a score,
and I guess he'd done that self-dividing thing himself

as I have: in the fingered press of muddled keys,
you lift your head and see the future rushing up –
illegible directions, a mess of threatening notes.

They say you can't think two things at the once:
the mind must flip from one thing to the next,
can't think Kyrie while you're singing Sanctus,

but I have played, inexpertly, piano.
There's your left hand and your right, conjoined
in playing the same piece, but separately,

as in the one Bach prelude I could almost play,
the slow-flowing burden, anchored in the left,
chasing those elusive patterns in the right.

III

The piano wavers, wows, does not ring true
although it is truthful; all the websites say
it is a faithful record of a wonky instrument.

The left hand wanders into eddies, languid drifts.
Above that there's the right hand's glittering rips,
runs of notes that pause then circle, run again.

I think he must think three thoughts while he plays:
in his left thick chords of gospel sashay on,
while his right contrives a song and plays along

and he listens for where the rivulet will flow:
what new idea or rhythmic turn he'll take
which must be drawn from what he's playing now –

half-glimpsed glints gathering towards the light
in the current's dimpled whirl and turbulence,
some new thing floating upwards to be born,

like the whisper of a neighbour's elm, the hiss
of Córdoba's fountains by the Alcázar,
a stream unfurls from what has gone before.

IV

The music rocks between two ancient chords
and the minor sequence fills with a regret
or loss he does not have to name, just play.

I think I hear a yearning, a nostalgic tone,
but that may be mine for those departed years,
for all that's lost, since I first heard this track;

but there's also future-loss, the still-to-come
which you and I won't speak of, or not yet,
which I hear in that Beethoven quartet –

we glance to the next page and we read sorrow;
play the vigorous opening, but in our playing
possessed also by that swift presentiment

of the slow movement, adagio non troppo,
singing regret for what we see must come,
singing regret for what we see must go.

Do not read the next page, live this as it comes,
running out and on from what has gone,
listening with me to Keith Jarrett at Cologne.

Space/Time

Hard-fisted summer incandesces at the windshield;
a breath of that bluster would whack you like a plank.

We surge across the Murray flood plains
pondering gravity waves as we drive –
a coupling of black holes collapse to one,
a billion years ago, a billion years away,
bending space to ruffle a photon beam
on Earth, like a platypus you do not see
but a ripple in a pool tells you it has been.

I tell my daughter tales of childhood holidays up here:

The dusty poplar avenue, leading to Tallangatta,
which even then was foundering in the rising lake,
when I was ten, muddy stumps knee deep in dam,
they're down there hoping for the end of days
to disinter them – when nothing hidden will stay hid;

at Cohuna, locals jump into the irrigation ditch –
fresh water! Danger! It won't let you float like salt,
I thought, or was it Dad restrained me? Skinny, pale,
he'd rarely swim – but, hells bells, he'd tell you how.

He'd rather a bold boy who'd leap into white water,
to someone who tried reading Proust in French,
one who'd pull a car apart for fun on Sunday,
and make a risky fortune trading real estate,
claiming our whole dry heat-laved land as his.

Although others peopled it for sixty thousand years
we looked upon the land and counted it as ours.
Its mysteries, like the footprint pebbles in the Ovens,
they were our mysteries, it was us who found them;
and before us there was nullity – the blank-time,
and chubby brown urchins painted on black velvet –
and there was no after, we were the summation,
we got sunburned and we won the Davis Cup.

By then the gravity wave had run a billion years
rippling galactic yachts, rocked them at their moorings,
and it would have passed through us and around us,
except it tangled in our photon beam, an instant;
then imperiously stepped on for someplace important –
the verges of blank-time, the last tick of space –
as we burn across the Murray floodplain summer.

Prelude to the Big Bang

I – Author's Note

don't get hung up on results, he says

but that's half of the fun, to think ahead
just how good it's going to be this time –
the swish of utmost modishness about it,
the parade of show-off stylish grandeur:

it will be as primeval as Genesis,
hair-raising as a shadow by your bed,
slouch across the page in long lines of slangy non sequiturs,
like Ashbery,
tangle from a thread
      f
       l
      u
       t
      t
      e
        r
      i
       n
        g
like a new leaf on an old tree

II – Overture – thinking of Haydn's Creation

darkness, on the deep,
formlessness, on earth

formless,

before chaos what?
unaskable question

what state preceded?
God blocks that ask

III – Before

(to the librettist)

begin
before beginning
write back before the before
prior to the drift of dark on waters
back prior before one
streak of wind
way back prior before
a strip of light
a spill of darkness
no water no ripple
beginning before beginning
before

(to the composer)

cease not
without beginning
eternal *ti*
forever promise
do
almost
about to
forever
ripening for
resolving
never

no when
no before
never after
never
culminating
nevermore

the opening gliss
to Rhapsody in Blue
but rise forever

make it so
you're not sure you heard
like a throat singer
hidden in a choir

IV – Smaller than an atom

See a world in a grain of sand,
cosmos in neutrino crammed.

It's still before day one began,
before the whole shebang began.

Stretching back to the long before
and waiting, for nothing, forevermore.

The jack-on-a-spring, its lid unlocked,
always about to ping from its box.

The bent bow, taut, compressed,
about to forever about to release.

Cellar door – Milawa

In Brown's long shed they unleash a gust of red
which whirls me back to Happy Valley one July
where the pruners crept along the trellises of neumes
like peasants of ill omen, wrapped against the cold,
while in the shed they pumped invisible shiraz
from barrel to oak barrel and I reeled
in the mingle of the ferment and vanilla fumes.

But here, now, with midsummer come, we pause
amongst these outrageous vines, this shining air,
and mind could lay aside its weary fret and blunder,
halt the clattering words, the torrent of remembrance,
could hold itself adroit and, balanced in the noon,
take hold, take hold of this…void, this hot silence.

Rapt – vine leaves bend blind faces to the sun,
absorbed in the great work, enchaining endless light,
beneath whose awful force they dip and lift,
perhaps as a moored boat on still water rides
an unseen ripple in time's flow and then subsides;
and not a midday bird that flits or ruffles, cries.

We have chanced upon a version of completion,
on this flood plain which mountains circle, still;
the grape paddocks covering miles, unmoving,
silent; of mower or of tractor no low drone,
no call of foreman to the labourers in the vineyard,
an absence greater than the sum of all subtraction.

All poems are liars

I was born one morning when a cosmic storm
made me caterwaul and pump my arms,
and rattle the shutters of the labour ward.
My father keenly sized me up and said:
he's gonna be a steel-driving man, Lord, Lord!

I grew up hearty, content to hit and mess
until some fool master showed me Keats
and I found I could ecstatically address
abstractions in a solemn frame of voice –
'Season of fruit and mellow wistfulness'.

When I was much older, I saw René Char
strike the blue and silver sparks that star
at the iron forge when he hammers words –
soft-handed, belatedly, I found I'm born
to die with my hammer in my hand, Lord, Lord!

On the beach

The far lick of this arc of beach is where
I sailed others' dinghies sixty years ago,
and knew that urgent clutch of joy, to clear
the sheltering bluff, into the open Bay,
spinnaker set shy in turbulent north wind,
heeling, hurtling over hull-slashed waves

sea-darkening squalls flay the flimsy craft;
a rush, a crack of sailcloth, all you sense
above the blustering wind about your ears,
the shock of salt spray on your naked chest.
What war was it then? The crisis over Cuba
when we slid out along obliteration's edge.

Two dark-capped terns slip solo down to bathe,
wingtip-flicking flashes in the rippling breaks
among a strut of matching silver gulls, but
give me terns, they hunt, no cadge, no whine.
They sweep the deep-etched reef, precise, then dive!
You fear they'll smash their elegance head on.

Airs frisk a silken innocence about you;
light haze blurs mild capes as they recede
into the clemency of early autumn noon,
northwards, where in a dazzling shimmer
the city towers, made spindly by the glare,
float above the merge of light and sea.

Further away, today, north-westerly and beyond,
are buildings bombed to wispy skeletons,
invisible across a half a globe, in dark.
No innocent airs across Ukraine this night.

Dear comrades

who fabricate our age's ruins-to-be:
super-arachnid cranes on wharves,
rusty ore piles, taller than pyramids,
falcon-nest offices which shine on our plains,
the cratered open cuts they see from space;

who coax our children through their sums,
trade ethereal currencies while we sleep;
who test millions of our samples overnight;
who tease thread and fabric into costume,
bejewel throats and wrists and breasts –

all I ever stitched were arguments for you,
which collapsed beneath us like a cavalry platoon
sent out to charge an ambuscade of guns.
I was loyal but I flexed, did what was possible,
worked the angles, dragging you from scrapes,
when I should be throwing spanners in the works.

Dear Victor Serge

Comrade, you went looking for trouble – save
that one night when you looked for medication
for your wife's fear something terrible would happen,
and Stalin's men seized you on your way home.

Cast out by the Soviets you lost everything,
carried West only what you held in your head:
the Milky Way glimpsed through a rusted roof,
four young women laughing as they ford a stream,

a child's kite soaring high above the steppe,
a warplane looping loops above the steppe
'along the golden fringes of white clouds',
and what you knew of the revolution's ruin.

Hand to mouth again, this time in Mexico,
you took a poem to show your son but found him
not at home, and put the poem in the post,
hailed a cab for home then died as you got in.

I fear I sense my end as I imagine yours:
We write and hope someday our children read us.
But as droplets slide across the silver weir
our words dash into turbulence and drown.

The use of travel

On and on through the woods to Chambord

Under the trees is almost as hot
as up on the windswept ridges where
cylindrical hay bales bake.

You wept for beauty as we rode
through the royal hunting park,
who don't weep at any stray feeling,

and any moment a magical stag
could catapult high across the path
with royal hounds in liveried pursuit.

It is immense when we get there
with the slate-roofed turrets gleaming,
the round towers bright with windows.

Henri comte de Chambord, long-time Claimant
rejected the chance to become King
unless the French gave up their tricolore.

He's on the screen in many ornate rooms
reciting his high lineage and grand schemes,
and coaches wait below to bear him to Paris.

I know commoners like Henri –
who on some point of principle
would haul the temple down about them

just to teach their boss a lesson,
or to expose a colleague's bad faith,
and demand I topple columns with them.

Henri, you've got it the wrong way round,
first you get to be king, then you change the flag!
But he would find that craven and tawdry

just like the commoners when I propose
they go north cane-cutting and fall in love,
give up justice and work up an honest sweat.

As we do in the forest of the would-be kings.

The way to Piediluco

At Assisi there's cold beer and a pizza tile
by the cathedral with its beggar at the door,
moaning, beset by each of Job's afflictions;
but we jostle to St Francis's basilicas.

Cimabue frescoes crumble to ghostly wrecks,
worn pallid in the press of priestly commerce.
But who am I to judge? Come to gawk and peer
like that man you found among the stony vines
on the door frame of St Francis' church at Todi,
sneaking to glimpse some prelate in his regalia,
but naked himself and the weather has unmanned him.

Then we roll back to Todi on the E45,
which unfurls like it's downhill all the way,
garlanded this morning by the holy chlorophyll
but overhung by storms now in the dusk.

All day today I've thanked those tourists yesterday,
near the cascades which flow only at appointed times,
who debated half an hour on how to split their bill
and held our waitress hostage so we missed the falls,
forcing us, for want of something else, to Piediluco

> where the hills glide into the encircled lake
> drawing down the chalky sky about them,
> and stands of poplars on the distant shore
> cast elegant likenesses upon the water,
> and from the wooded tributary vales
> flows a secret quiet, enfolding every sound.

Foreseen at Victor Harbour

A swan wallows in the break,
bedraggled, all at sea –
its head above the turmoil,

its body, a string bag
stuffed with feather dusters,
tumbles in white water.

Now it's dragged among green peaks,
to eye collapsing rollers
in breathless catastrophe.

The swan must look out for itself –
Four riders, like the end of days,
bear at full gallop down on us.

I pull my fledglings back towards the dunes,
hoisting the littlest in my arms,
glad her mother doesn't know the threat

I brought her child to, as she sleeps;
though I have reason to foretell
that it is for her the hooves toll.

Death of Ulysses

Tongued flames crown him flickering as he speaks.
Dante damns him to this hell, then questions –
how does he come here, how he met his end –
by going where mankind was never meant to go,
by seducing those rough innocents, his loyal crew.

Primo Levi, in another circle of the damned,
plays Italian teacher to a young French Jew
as they stumble, slowly as they dare, with a stick
on their shoulders, to balance cabbage soup,
and Primo dredges fragments of Dante, to teach.

Ulysses veers his prow towards Gibraltar
sails past the Pillars and on through empty seas
south to where he sights a mountain grey with distance.
(Primo falters here as he recalls the peaks
where he joined the partisans to end in Auschwitz.)

A savage whirlpool takes hold of the ship,
hollow seas close above Ulysses and his crew,
and Primo founders as he navigates this verse,
living where humans were not meant to go,
seas closing on him, as the Almighty planned.

Ordained

The Good Lord yanked the pinball plunger
hard against the spring and let it whack!
shooting particles upon the flashing field of play,
outwitting entropy, abhorring vacuums,
past blazing canyons of black holes
and slung from one wide orbit to the next.

He knew what would befall them one and all,
each of their furthest consequences –
down to the escape of the superb blue wren
hunted in the hedge by our marmalade Fred,
and the denting of the car which skittled him,
teaching my daughter something more of grief.

Although Dante's All-Seeing Eye sees all
what It sees is not required to happen.
From our headland we foresee a racing yacht
capsize in a ferocious gust and break
a crewman's leg, whose kids must go
without their fish and chips while he's laid low.

If We, All-seeing, foresaw these consequences,
would We not bend the rush of that same gust
towards another vessel, to the one that's sailed
by a broker, versed in the surge of market forces,
able to turn to profit any twist of any gale,
and spare those poor children their deprivation?

Let the broker sustain a twisted arm
and leave the driving to his learner son,
who turns into a side street by mistake,
with the purr of Dad's Mercedes in his ears,
and without a second thought will crush
an orange cat and save a superb blue wren.

On water

Match racing off the quay at Malmö –
two catamarans burn down a spinnaker run,
careering almost abreast to the mark –

fast boats, sharp boats, giving no quarter,
they would have been devilish
in battles on the Öresund,

flying through on one foaming hull,
quicker with fire and axe and death
than even Vikings could conceive.

They race against the bridge from Denmark,
suspension cables strung behind them.
Ice-cream parlour awnings rattle.

Back seventy years these were working docks
on those hard nights when Danes sailed Jews
across the strait and Gestapo hunted.

I come from a fearful, pitiless nation;
however blond and fortunate Swedes are
their parents welcomed fugitives by water.

Swedish for travellers

First I heard the music of her –
the telltale Viking run and lilt,
then she commandeered my sight,
photographing Monet's *nymphéas*
as though she was free, alone
of all us intruders into Paris,
to plunder photons from great works.

Next day we're shopping in Printemps,
but none of their clothes will ever go
with a lumpy, sore-backed, limping man.
I stop and wait at the escalators' foot
amongst the dazzling accessories,
and down she glides, with the same tilt
as yesterday, but more fluent,
without her long-lensed SLR to heft.

God dag! I'm damn near delighted into saying,
as if my meagre Swedish had not fled,
as if sharing Monet had formed a bond,
as if I am as memorable as her.

In Todi I sit way up the endless flight
of wide-stretched steps to the Franciscan church,
and watch a woman climb towards me,
in the automatic male way that could enrage her,
but when she's on my step, she says *God dag!*
and settles her pack with two rapid shrugs
while I scrabble about my Swedish, finding
smör och bröd, and *varmt och skönt* –
bread and butter, or warm and pleasant,
and by then she has passed me by –
tongue-tied with inappropriate phrases.

The Vikings harried Paris plenty. I had heard
about the famous Danish band who heaved
their long-boats cross-country on their backs
to the River Marne when the Seine was chained.
A teacher told me, when he heard me drag my heels,
hoping to inspire me to a manly tread.

Long time since – the teacher, the Vikings,
fine-looking Swedish travellers, their walk,
but Monet's ponds and water-lilies gleam
towards an answering glimmer deep in me.
I gasp with an animal, a fundamental, awe,
in an oval room beside the once-barred Seine.

Another country

Two days on the trail and I'm lost in pilgrim thought;
all I dreamed last night was where to find stout boots.

Town alleys twist and merge, they mean to lead astray;
better the trail which winds and climbs but tends our way.

The trail is headlong, downward; stones we've trod pelt past;
each next step we attempt is impeded by the last.

Ah! There's birdsong and the path leads down in shade,
but a pilgrim's yellow cross tells us that way is barred.
The way is hard to find and when it's found it's hard.

The pilgrim signs point us to the Bridge of Risk It All –
I ventured on it once before and lived to tell the tale
but my partner in that wager she did not fare so well.

*

At first I did not dream I could survive this long;
but the stony rise is steep; sore-pawed I must slope on.

What harm could befall me at the Fountain of the Wolf?
The waters may enchant me into a joyous whelp.

Prowling in the night I pass the sound of bright guitars,
at a lighted window someone shouts ¡Hola!
I hide here in the dark to steal the words of their coplas.

*

Out of the light the cavers swing into my buried soul;
all they'll find down here is rock and barren walls.

Seven strokes fall from the faint bell in its tower,
it rings out all my decades and then tolls no more.

Behind my back the stealthy dawn turns day to light.
The world outside can wait; I face the dark and write.

*

First English and then Huguenots broke through its walls,
now besieging treetops beset it on its hill
but our pale stone township holds out still.

Three towers, a baker, a church if you're prone to sin
or sit in the sun-spill square and drink sharp wine.

Saturday, the market stalls are piled high in the square;
there's wine and empanadas, fruit and capacious bras;
a busker sings like Brel; pretend we come from here.

*

As we walked along the wooded ridge a bell rang thirteen;
nothing else was untoward, it was a magic afternoon.

In the deserted chapel the bell ropes gently swing –
Our two paths brought us here in time to ring fourteen.

A teasing hint of beyond thrown down by coloured glass;
reach for it and it slips like quicksilver from your glance.

Along the rough hedgerow, beside the ploughed lands,
across the dappled stream to slopes striped by vines,
the trail brings us free, the walls of Eden are thrown down.

Cannaregio

Foam wake glimmers on the dim canal;
barges and ferries forge,
       bright-lamped,
beneath the brick arched bridge and me,
shaking for want of sleep, at dawn.

The skipper of a barge controls the helm
between his knees and balances
       against
the wash of wavelets, rolls a cigarette,
shouts directions to his scrawny mate.

He must have someone ashore, who bills
merchants and wholesalers –
       his wife perhaps
canvassing for work, grown thin with chasing debts,
finding cash for moorings, permits, repairs;

but he's on board, between arrival and depart,
weighed to the waterline with
       groceries and wine,
or staggering with a cargo of cement and steel,
his mortgaged bow above the waves, for now.

Venice for diverse instruments

Perhaps a secret joy is needed to write a poem? – Victor Serge,
Notebooks, 25 March 1941

Downstairs in my sounding house my daughter practised flute,
running solo lines until they rippled ribbon in the air
and summoned the foundling girl Vivaldi wrote them for,
who tapped the felted keys as nimble-fingered as my girl,
giving her eager little gasp after each long-breathed phrase.

When we got to Venice you and I took breakfast in a bar
where I envied the bold natives who prepare the day ahead
with a white wine or Campari set before them on the zinc;
or maybe they'd had their day – on their barges before dawn
hauling groceries and wine – and stepped in, for just the one.

Set my funeral there with off-duty cooks and *vaporetto* crew,
women come from market, receptionists and string quartets
off to play for tourists, and I will grace the sad event.
Have them play the buoyant piece that makes me a Venetian,
and from some *fondamenta*, launch me with Vivaldi in my sails.

Had we but world enough

I knew a woman, lovely in her bones,
When small birds sighed, she would sigh back at them;
Ah, when she moved, she moved more ways than one:
The shapes that a bright container can contain!

Theodore Roethke, 'I knew a woman'[1]

Gloss on lines by Roethke

Outside the Tardis bento place I halt,
tipsy with green tea and infused with you,
and watch you strike, all business, back to work
at how your denim skirt, cut on the bias,
swirls flamenco ripples round your runner''s legs.
Turn back! I want to catch you up and take you home
and twirl you in this line I've known for years
which tangled me straight off on my first read,
I saved it till I snared an athlete for my own –
'I knew a woman, lovely in her bones'.

That denim skirt was our first year, the start
of our millennium, our supernova burned,
but we went slow enough to illustrate Marvell,
who you were sure was a predatory sleaze.
I blamed the nuns who taught you – how could they
condone two hundred years spent on each breast,
and how did they explain, how could they not condemn,
what happens in 'thirty thousand for the rest'?
In bed at last we'd vegetable company –
your neighbour's elm used Roethke's stratagem:
When small birds sighed, she would sigh back at them.

Am I shallow, I've asked us many times, are you?
So much of our meaning lies in food and drink –
tapas, *i cicchetti,* sushi, wine – that bar
in side-street Madrid. But one afternoon in bed,
in aftermath, I saw my tears glint in your hair,
flesh of my flesh, I said, bone of my bone –
and like Adam felt the uttermost of kinship stir –
that was not shallow; I was way beyond my depth.
Oh, I was moved, and remembered Roethke's line:
Ah, when she moved, she moved more ways than one.

From Lisbon you slept all night on the all-night train,
but, being wired to hyper-vigilant, I kept watch –
past trackside junkyards lit by fires in drums,
with shadow guards, but as we neared Madrid
my thought flew to Atocha, not far up the line,
which they bombed in the year that we first came;
then my mind rushed on to Córdoba at midnight,
flamenco in the water gardens, when your head
dreamt on my shoulder all the brilliant stars of Spain –
The shapes that a bright container can contain!

Atocha 2004

Rumbling through the outskirts in the early dawn,
on the all-night train from Lisbon to Madrid,
still gloomy, so that in the auto wrecking yards
and encampments the braziers burn bright.
I think of commuters who check the time and yawn,
but in the station up ahead they'll be blown apart.

When they bombed Atocha we were safe at home
but preparing our first journey into Spain,
and our friends asked us if we'd 'cut and run' –
mimicking machismo of the Australian Right
still glorying in the capture of Baghdad.
But not to go would feel like giving in.

We've run to see Guernica, eaten our paella,
now we're at Atocha six months beyond the blast,
eager for Catalonia and France ahead.
Tourists clamour to board the train to Barcelona,
enraged by the blocking Guardia and his gun,
but surrounded by all Spain's silent dead.

Proposal

I send you this message, in a little dream train –
two-foot long, maybe eight inches high,
rattling on its narrow gauge along
the railway easement, by the cemetery wall,
I send to ask, again, if we can wed.

What if my older daughters should find this?
They think three marriages enough, they think
my car, which you say must last until I die,
should shuttle wearily from here to you,
wearing out its life in pointless little trips.

Your dishwasher would swish for you alone,
and my cookbooks, gathered from Barbados
to Ceylon, would be only mine, but rarely used,
not jostling with your modish ones on shelves
in some shared future crowded house.

While Reading Flow Chart

I drowse, and there they are, a century ago,
people I can't know, serious, removed,
scanning bills of lading, shipping manifests,
trading cargo brought in from the East,
taking tea with fathers-in-law to be.

It's all worked out, alliances are made,
the daughters bluntly told their happy fate,
the ceremonial fabrics ordered in,
the lists of guests composed, small mansions leased,
the young men's mistresses bad brusque farewell.

Then, with formalities properly observed,
returned from horse-drawn honeymoon resorts,
young women gaze in sun-filled airy rooms,
as grey dust settles thick upon their shelves,
and years of marriage decorously sift down.

Thunder early Saturday

Something woke me
Saturday 'round daybreak;
then all birdsong all at once.

The light has a lulling glamour
like it glances from a moat,
mottled as rippled water;

far away an iron water tank
tumbles down a granite hill;
like army tanks across a metal bridge

or naval cannon practice
in my childhood, in peacetime,
bar Korea, Suez, Malaya, Indochina.

Dissident suburbs to our east
are bombarded by dry thunder;
we're left alone, for now.

There are few enough good dawns –
one in a stone cabin in the Luberon,
one on the walls of an Etruscan town,

one in a makeshift bed and breakfast
in the hills, where each bird hunts
something smaller than itself to kill.

Just now maybe hell broke loose
but somewhere elsewhere,
leaving us in peace, for now

Lavender

The green whiff of pruning, the shears' clip,
summon Mrs Malcolm from across the road
to cut Mum's Easter daisy back to naught.
'You're too kind, Bunny,' she says to Mum
and whistles or whispers as she lays about,
head level with her widespread knees,
a prayer to her tough gardener's god:

> 'O Lord, I offer up this pruning, this
> pang in my countrywoman's back.'

My hedge grew from a memory of Provence,
the tang of wild herbs on rocky trails,
walking those dry mountainsides with you –
ruffled lanterns, waist-high, glow
above the woody sprawl, incense

> our veranda, consecrate it
> to a fierce midsummer god.

Off with their long-stalked heads,
their last bees still sluggishly about them –
snip after clip I nudge towards
the idea of roundedness,

> those long mounded strips
> on southward facing slopes.

Now I tread profusion that I've slaughtered,
trampling flower heads like the fallen hair
when I shaved Susanne's head during chemo

> her dark curls falling at my feet
> to grow back more luxuriant,
> and give the seeming of false hope.

Grevillea

This day we wandered gardens with our friends
and I captured this grevillea going mad,
glowing profusion in grey Sunday air.
You three gardeners crunched the gravel paths,
and I fell behind you, covering ground
ungainly, with a tendency to weep.

I snapped it quick, without a forethought,
caught something that I didn't know was there,
as unseen ghosts appear to mist the film.
Woven through that wayward random sprawl,
hidden by its thoughtless flourishing,
netted by its tracery of shade and light,
present, out of sight, this winter's day
is abundant earth's heedless self-delight.

In dreams let us not use first names

Jim's here, who I haven't seen awake for decades,
and tries to scare me that they'll rip off our hands;
but as soon as he's said that he's gone, and I peer
in a gloomy barn decked out for a travelling show,
like when I was a kid at the Mechanics Institute
with the whip-cracking skimpy cowgirl and her dog,
and there he is sprawled in a bean bag
craning his whiskery neck, the way he does
and waving his white splay-fingered hands at me.

The barn is done up as a disused fairground,
a Ferris wheel unmoving in a starry painted sky,
canvas shutters on the sideshows drawn down tight
and the surprised clown heads revolve invisibly
referring to some noir film or Pablo Fanque's Fair.

Ah here we bloody go! Bright young pairs of men
in uniform, like military, but really ushers
from the old-time movies, dance à la Busby Berkley,
and upon the air there's a disembodied voice
spruiking an impresario with a toffy name,
a pretentious name, Gervais Dalrymple perhaps.

I go outside to find my wife, and there she is,
conversing with some stranger there, one of them,
and dressed in one of their uniforms, with shirt and tie.
I'm so wild with her for being part of their scene
that I turn away fumbling for my cigarettes.
She's found someone else, some superior
scourge of middle-class lowbrows like me.

Some tart-tongue is wagging in my head:

After forty years of a pretty satisfactory marriage,
after raising their kids and wheedling them out of home,
after making love every Sunday afternoon
with his tall, stern wife looming above him,
after he made her pot roast and brown gravy,
who couldn't lie down for fear of reflux,
it would end because she fell in love with theatre.

But it will end because these players have exposed me –
my jealousy, my stodginess, my timid envy –
all in their devil-may-care, polished accents.
I know what I'm like, but everyone else didn't have to.

An extended simile runs out of puff

To Graham

As a summer southerly blows up the Bay
upsets giddy dinghies racing at Rosebud,
rips gaudy spinnakers into bright tatters,

yelps at container ships slow in the channel
blusters at gantries gathered in posses,
dockside, on the mud-sluggish river;

then browbeats barristers' chambers on William,
whistling at corners and whining at counsel
until the falcons go hunting for shelter;

and blusters northwards over the flat lands
to where a grim vigneron watches it coming,
anxious for fruit in his Macedon vineyard –

so did our book group burst on our quarry
beset them and best them, all the great works;
leaving them bottled, swamped by our boldness.

We demanded they face your implacable question:
Do they tell us how to live a good life?
And many, it seemed, would rather not answer.

We took Virgil's measure, but that night was sad,
you'd sprung our friend from his ward to join us;
he was failing, good luck we'd Aeneas to talk of.

61

Then he, our gentle co-reader, died.
I can see his benign canny gaze as he looks
across Taradale hills for glimpse of his Christ.

It's time he sent us one of his emails
spruiking the latest to win the Nobel,
or a novel so worthy we just have to read it

but any message would do, from wherever –

Miss Agda – Wild Strawberries[2]

Ample and prickly, you tuck Professor into bed,
who is beat, his ancient battery flat.

A harpist lightly thumbs a ripple down her strings,
his cousin glissandos to him down the enervating years,
who he loved and lost and pined for ever since,
which you don't hear but you nod, your task being done,
having brusquely overseen descent of peace.

First time I watched this scene I sweetly wept;
he had earned his peace – long life and hard day.

You've lulled him helplessly beyond awareness:
of his remote son's bleak dislike, and of his own
neglect of those most in need of his comfort,
while he's kind to strangers with the easiest old charm,
which brings to mind my children's father and my own.

You bring to mind, white hair grabbed tightly back,
rustic apron starched and billowy, those country aunts,
when the family gathered and forced me on the floor,
who seized me in the barn dance to their floral breasts,
and whirled me saying —'You're Cliff's boy? You've grown!'
and spun off, while I watched my cousin twirl
progressing to me round the circle of the dance;
who'll now be billowy and old as you are, Agda.

Today I changed a tyre and felt a tremor of my age.
I almost gave it up, but the Professor – he surrenders,
as the corpse's hand draws him to a coffin in his dream.
Let that not be me surveying life receding,
falling blissfully asleep into doddery acceptance.

My mum shuddered when her friends looked forward to
    their deaths,
'I don't look forward to it, son, at all,' and yet she managed.
Going ahead of me, dry fingers fretting at her rosary.
But I am not yet brave enough to die.

March 2020

Enter the balloons – arranged in elegant relation
to cranes and factories, hoardings, shining towers –
travellers in baskets, hung from bladders of hot air.

They slide above the bluestone church with spire,
above our shallow valley – the town hall clock,
terraces, apartments, shops – a graceless jumble.

We farewelled a public man there at the church,
this time last year, the most decent man I think I knew,
remained my friend, long after he had reason.

There were good people amongst our enemies
he would tell me – he had found them to be so –
'Just so long as you are with them,' I would think.

I saw him last ten years ago – another funeral,
another church, another death; him cancer-frail;
we barely spoke, there was too much to tell.

I look to the balloons from behind our double glaze –
They go not where they list but where winds will,
over hotels, hospitals and nursing homes; they drift.

They say the cancer wrung him hard in those last years,
relentless, ever harder. Suppose that's how it goes –
the most generous meet the least scrupulous foe.

Talking back

Great-grandfather Henry was a bankrupt,
the coroner was told he wandered and was vague.
His descendants were numerous and fertile
and we spread across the land like plague.

Bealiba

By the river, in the Great War, there's a shot
of infant Dad sat in a tub for his wash
outside the family tent. How did our dad get
to be so helpless and how did that soft
child become our cranky domineering cuss?

A hundred years ago my granddad led
a work crew, as *Bealiba Times* records,
sent to drill for gold. Grandma soon bore Dad,
and then the older children – Zillah, Ced –
appear in the *Times* winning school awards.

Our dad's centenary will lack his attendance –
'What about him are you going to celebrate?'
My wife drills in me for a seam of repentance,
who showed her own father a forbearance
and tenderness I cannot duplicate.

Not his offers to wield the noose instead
of a hangman, if one could not be found –
but how he'd squat by a built-up garden bed,
take a fistful of the soil he'd worked and fed,
and let it tumble through his fingers to the ground.

Not his dismissal of Picasso or Cézanne
but the way he wondered at the gift of sight –
he'd shake his head and knowing that you can
never really pin it down, he would return
to his amateur painter's wrestle with the light.

Bluff

Crumbling rusted-ochre cliff face, stacked
above a blackened base of fallen rock.
You painted that bluff how many times?

Attempted its clouds, which would not stand
for any Sunday painter to perfect them,
milky laundry, pegged to catch the light.

Smaller it seems than a heap of builder's sand
but once bulked, shoulder hunched at Bay,
the southern buttress of our seaside world.

We both painted Sunday nights, that year
when I swapped chemistry for art and worked
in the kitchen, with you also painting there

and I don't recall either of us made remark
on what the other painted – me befuddled
in some maladroit attempt to mimic Braque

and you, despising Braque and maybe me,
I thought, and working on your bluff,
amid your oils and turpentine and fags.

Now it is promontories, capes, which draw me,
the misted folds of ridges one behind another
the craggy outline of your bluff against the blue.

Mothers' Beach

Ken in my watercolour class is painting
Mothers' Beach, following a painting
by a well-known artist I don't know.

His is really not the beach I knew
and scorned (because who would be seen
dead on Mothers' and Babies' Beach?).

You can't see the park where one Sunday
some boys met a girl from the Catholic school.
They wondered about her Monday morning –

Did she have a bra on under that sweater?
A thought I wasn't allowed to think
which seized me like a feverish invasion.

Ken brushes white paint on an edge
of card and presses it onto his art
to leave an imprint of white masts

made spindly by distance and by sun glare.
It is a wonderful trick and I'll use it soon
in a seaside painting of my own.

I grew up there, I tell Ken, as though
that's something that will weigh with him –
that I know well the beach he's painting.

But to Ken where I grew up, and whether
she had a bra, is of no account,
less than a salt-bleached feather.

White gull

This is your parents' room where the battered table
grows with the cranking of a handle
and I crouch behind Grandad's chair and try
to unpick his pencil notes on Darwin.

The print on the chimney turns the room to sad.
It must be Scotland where Grandma comes from:
black cliffs dive to a deadly churning sea
and the gale buffets one white gull.

You argue with Grandad about Einstein,
whether you can draw an infinitely small
triangle around an infinitely small point,
and your voice is harsh for dismissing fancy

like the day I asked about the three little pigs –
whether the wolf could hear them talk through glass;
or when I'd learned about Bishop Berkeley
and goaded you with his assault on common sense.

Grandad didn't seem to mind – maybe he enjoyed
having his youngest son to bamboozle.
He didn't need my support from behind his chair
who sounded like he never lost an argument.

Despite your scorn for fancy, you would talk
into your eighties about quarks to any moth
who fluttered unwary within your shrunken reach,
hoping to trap in controversy any passing son.

Portrait with Australian Birds

I – Australian White Ibis

Somewhere in the northeast
a road dips through parched lands
to a willow-shaded creek.

You wave us to silent awe.
White priests process –
ibis along the stream.

It was ten years since
you came forth from Egypt,
sent home from the war.

Maybe ibis were consecrate
from those air force days
tending the war birds

with a fag hung from your lip
or maybe all birds were sacred –
come from beyond this brutal world

where a flimsy crate could flip
nose first into the airstrip
and the youthful pilot burn.

II – Spur wing plover

You wake under canvas
vacant night is wide about you,
in that wavering moment
between sleep and awake,
uncertain if outside is desert
and you are camped in Egypt
by your airfield, and should strain
for the drone of enemy bombers,
or if the whisper is the Bay
breathless under press of starlight.
Then you catch the high stabbing
plover's cry, lonely, from the sky.
Its lamentation falls on you.

III – White-faced heron

May be seen in a grey coat,
its drab fisherman's garb,
anywhere bright water shines
where a salesman might stop
his car and watch him fish.

Four years after Dad had gone
a white-faced heron stalked
across my brother's lawn
creakily, as though each step
it was about to grab its back

to ease some long-time ache
and cry some cranky cuss.
The soul does transmigrate!
Here's proof beyond a doubt.
Dad's here for a beer with us.

Maundy Thursday, Westernport

This sky is advertisement for painting classes:
to the west veils over ragged veils of grey
drape and dim a cavernous bright dome,
and southwards thumb-smeared streaks,
of almost rain, smudge the merge of sea and sky.

This beach, the island blurred across the strait,
would draw you – and the gallant fishing boat
that ploughs its white-flecked way to where you worked
on the timber bridge, and bought that block of land,
adrift in grass and waited to get rich; and waited

Too soulful, you might have said about this dusk
as you said of a Spanish mass another day –
if you were here to paint it, if you were not
dead and buried twenty miles away.
Too soulful – the end of day, withdrawing light.

Where the light goes

My father stared an autumn afternoon,
self-wrapped in his meagre sheet, enthralled
by the window brimming light in his high room;
it was his last autumn, they were his last hours –
wind propelled a branch and clouds and hauled,
straight to his painter's eye, the scudding light.

Now here's his great granddaughter swaddled tight,
I glance into her room from the dim hall,
a bundle turned to face a curtained window's glow.
She's still, her dark eyes fasten on the bright
which has absorbed her through to shadow fall;
she charges herself, she fills herself with light.

This must be how Zen monks began,
bound on their mother's back in a rough shawl,
they too were struck by that transfixing glow –
which as full-grown masters they find within
when they cast their nets, drag in their haul,
too dim to grasp, grand slippery light.

Pandemic

The poet must keep an equal balance between the physical
world of waking and the terrible ease of sleep[3]

Equal balance

I test my life between a thumb and finger when I wake:
It is meagre, soon you will shoot peas through it,
as our parents said of a flimsy argument or dress,
like the sacks when I cleaned beaches, weave agape

There is a villainous ceiling of dark cloud with curtains
of fierce mist descending. Wind thuds the window.
I know, as we do in dreams, that it is storming
in my hometown – that it is wild like here.

'As we do in dreams,' I said, foolishly –
of all the unknowables this is the ultimate –
I cannot know what it is like in your dream;
more chance of knowing the bliss of saints.

'Little moon! Little moon!' I bay to our cold neighbour,
but it's like my vocal cords are cut, like a noisy dog's.
That's how it works, isn't it – the harsher the rebuff
the more desperate our attachment to the gods?

I dared the forces of galactic evil to attack our planet,
to force the gods to unveil themselves, protect us.
Don't ask me why I thought the gods are on our side;
it's one of those assumptions you make in dreams.

You know something's happening

The Second Coming came, a pastor announced
but went unnoticed, with everything that's going on.
A huckster's trick – assert what cannot be disproved –
last week the rule of Antichrist and kindred beasts began,
a brush with genius changed the heart of Kim Jong Un.

But the thick-embroidered world appears no more worn
or radiant than it has these last four billion years,
and it looks like it's got billions more to run,
although litter whirls with a self-possessed aplomb,
as if humans may not be in charge for long.

Outside things go hard. Some of our children
are out of work, others are at risk at work.
Everyone agrees that everything has changed.
They say we can't go back to how things were,
for good or ill, the milk can't be unspilt, although
kings sat on their thrones long after the Black Death.

On the left we've learned to value mutual kindness,
we don't survive alone we say, we need each other,
we need epidemiologists and masks and guinea pigs.
The other side has learned the opposite – they say
that (unlike them) the old were always going to die
and we should loose the hounds of selfishness.

Who'd have guessed there's so much rage in us?
That all we desire is to live and die in rancour?

Between the last tram and the first

I mend a spoiled painting,
repaint in my dark thought –
a low green wave breaks almost
against a thumb-smudged sky
above a streaked and silvered strait

the hours of sirens and the muffled clack
of traffic signals for the blind –
that rapid flicking on a rusty can

the pubs are locked again
the yelling, boisterous and sad,
no longer roam our laneways.
You'd reckon you could sleep

you won't catch it with dabs and flicks:
the poise of the next wave as it peaks,
light winking at its toppling crest
about to become what it was sent to be

but someone must keep watch
wake and stare in the swarming dark

an indolent gesture of a wave
a pulse from someplace placid
barely rising before it subsides
a very few molecules displaced
some photons shimmying aside
from its careless breaking almost

in the dead hours after the last tram.

Anniversary 2021

Ah them, they say of us. They go way back,
to the turn of the millennium, you know!
You can see the years begin to tell on him
but she looks like she's really got some go!

It's true, you still are supple as a reed.
When we take our walk you draw ahead,
I watch your stylish hair, your springy stride,
and your sweet feet rapid in lascivious red.

We've lasted long enough for you to hold
your head high with your long-married kin.
You've nothing left to prove, just leave me here,
kick up your scarlet heels, go out and sin.

Or don't – stay home, chuck your red shoes
off the nearest bridge on the sparkling Yarra.
Sit down on our designer couch with me
fire up the big TV and watch our *Vera*.

I'm not allowed out to fetch you flowers,
nor you to buy my watercolour set,
they won't release us to a slap up dinner;
this year this poem's all you get. Pet.

Riot

1

Proud boys in high vis and anti-capsicum bandanas
pass in ungainly clumps along our tramlines,
ahead of them cops backpedal in lime vests,
and behind they're trailed by more bright police
trundling a watchful rearguard at their heels.

They don't march for the right to seek asylum,
but for lunch huts to shelter from the storm;
not for freedom from the fear of torture,
but the citizens' right not to bare their arms.
They're against masks or vaccines, fear of virus,
but before they march frock up in safety gear.

This is why we left our spring streets empty? To let
these lumpen fuckers flock about ad libitum,
thump the cops, kick stray dogs, spit on nurses,
and call upon the rest of us to 'do your research!'.

Roxanne shouts across to the tram tracks
'You stupid fuckers! I hope you all get Covid',
but doesn't mean it – we know a lovely nurse
works triage. We don't want her swarmed
by the ignorant, the angry, the infected-on-principle.

2

On his retirement Zoom John prefigured this –
recalling marching against the Vietnam War,
with old blokes yelling curses from the footpath,
a damned sight younger than he and I are now.

Ten years later John's at work in Frankston –
only place in this state they read the Riot Act,
at the cop shop near the crossroads with three pubs,
which I passed through, hitching, many a time.

Newspapers suggest police detained a 'cripple'
– that's what they said – who they believed was drunk,
and all the lads went on a righteous rampage,
which shines a more benign light on a riot.

Then I drift off to before John and Vietnam,
to the Matthew Flinders cinema in Mornington,
where, at the end, they play 'God Save the Queen',
and I, of course, stand dutiful in my place,

but nearby a leather-jacket bloke just sits,
his hair swept back in an Elvis kind of swirl,
and when a tweedy squatter demands he stand
he points to the bodgie legs he does not have.

Some meek thing stirs within me, I'm on his side –
against the respectable who order cripples about,
and the proud boys, too, who are content to leave
the old and infirm, disabled, in pandemic's tracks.

Letters to New England

To Dugald Williamson

Prologue

You gave me the idea that we might sit
beside your fire and talk about our verse –
why we write poems, what's the point of it,
about line and rhythm, rhyme and assonance,
what we believe in, how politics can fit.
It would take weeks to trek this universe,
>   my thoughts rushing out from where they've amassed,
>   these fifty years since our student era passed.

There'd be New and Collecteds all over the place,
as we reached down our touchstone works to read –
I want to go back to that passage in Yeats,
whose run is so subtle the rhyme isn't heard;
and that echo of your sharp, oblique grace,
which I hear in Emily Dickinson's work.
>   But that won't be soon, I'm Covid-confined.
>   I will try to write you what's on my mind.

Letter One – Constrained

I had thought to emulate Lord Byron
by writing to you in this rhyming schema,
a form avoided later by brisk Auden
who, when headed northwards on a steamer,
(for Byron's Venice substituting Iceland)
affected Byron's nonchalant demeanour;
      but these first stanzas show it's hard to beat
      my thoughts into the scheme and make them fit.

He's not high in moral standing but I find,
as I contort my thought for rhyming verse,
that Ezra Pound comes frequently to mind,
who says in his 'ABC' that writers must
keep their eyes on their object, not let the line
be tempted by the pretty play of words.
      I write grandchildren's limericks and see
      rhyme draws me where I hadn't thought to be.

That may not be precisely what Pound said
but I dare not look it up exact, for fear
I must rewrite it – must unpick the thread,
and find I'd lose a rhyme I bled for there.
There are recent Nobel laureates as bad –
Bob Dylan grabs for any rhyme that's near:
      don't ask him if the game is worth a candle,
      he must shackle Handel with a Vandal.

Milton, although he wrote his share of rhymes,
said many poets, due to rhyme's constraints,
have exprest themselves often otherwise,
and for the most part worse, than how they meant
their thought to go when they began their lines,
in that pre-verbal nudge of first intent.
>   For his godly epic he threw rhyme over –
>   and was right, just try to read Pope's Homer.

I feel like an imposter when I rhyme,
I'm nimbler, less susceptible to gloom,
and there's a slapstick subtext every time
I manage to avoid impending doom
and prestidigitate some word which chimes
with an unlikely one – say Saskatoon.
>   Rhyme, it can be said, and I will fly this kite,
>   sets Verse on wings toward the realms of Light.

And five-stress lines – I find they lack for space.
I've schooled myself for years to stretch lines out,
hoping to give my thought more room to pace,
deploring this glib, summed-it-all-up sound,
this verbal dressage managed with prim grace,
treading and retreading trodden ground.
>   Now I revisit your much shorter lines
>   and marvel how much more's in them than mine.

Letter Two – About words

Do poems bubble up with spontaneous rush,
dazzling forth demanding to be written?
Should their manner imitate how feelings dash –
glancing, fluid, skipping on unbidden
not bound by any syntax we can guess,
curling round deep secrets they keep hidden?
>> I've been reading Alice Oswald's wondrous Dart;
>> it is all that and premeditated art.

That is a fork I come often to confront,
it's a railway switch, it's an either/or:
attempt to mimic the initial glint,
reflect vivid in extemporary form?
or set a straitening cage about the hint
of insight, the donnée I started from?
>> This time, through my choice of this tight stanza,
>> the straitening, encaging, track's my answer.

There's another question. I can't really tell
how well it squares with that preceding verse –
can we strike truth like a spark from a nail?
making the poem a hammer at the forge,
or do we accept that words are all talk,
and hope that in talking truth will emerge,
>> in heightened speech? As I struggle to say
>> what it's like, far past the middle of my way.

Some say they're writers because they love words!
I doubt that they've ever attempted a clause
which holds fast, won't slip from better to worse
when it's parsed by a lawyer for some boss.
They leave gnawed bones where you'd written plump birds,
as they transmute your workers' gold to dross.
>   Words wear, they fade, won't stand still on one spot –
>   I can't say I love them but they're what I've got.

My mistrust of the materials we use –
sign feebly tied to shadowy signified –
betrays me to a nihilist disgust.
My works, and others' works that I've admired,
collapse, deflate, like tents without a post,
I gaze upon a barren countryside –
>   Like Peggy Lee I ask 'Is that all there is?'
>   When all is said and summed, it comes to this?

Letter Three – In Paradisum

One Sunday concert on the radio,
there's something, maybe by Rachmaninov,
makes my parents differ, as they often do.
Dad says technique is all he's thinking of,
Mum hears only emotion's ebb and flow –
they talk while it plays, it's Rimsky-Korsakov,

       his lonely violin – *Scheherazade*,
       it's Sinbad, far from any friendly harbour.

Dad's voice would catch over chord progressions
in 'Sweet and Low', from his days in a choir,
he was a fraud to disavow emotions;
but Mum – for once I wouldn't follow her,
no detail, only sweeping imprecisions.
It was all about how different they were –

       The bloke must be practical, pragmatic,
       the woman was intuitive, romantic.

Not long before she died my mum confessed
unease to have a son approaching sixty,
but she was gone a year before the guests
came to celebrate that awkward birthday.
My speech recollected how my parents pressed
their contradictory values on me –

       how they forced me to try to reconcile
       feeling with making, and subject with style.

Few parents could have given better gifts
but often it's hard to know who to blame –
like when Fauré's *In Paradisum* lifts
my earthbound bass's soul beyond mundane,
I find, my entrance come, that I emit
a tearful squawk and turn away for shame.

> Am I moved by doctrine I used to believe,
> or how the sopranos and the organ weave?

Letter Four – On form and content

The Bauhaus said that function equals form,
and form, us modernists were taught, must fit
the content, though we believe it's flawed
to see the form as something that's distinct,
like a bucket in which meaning can be poured,
which holds its shape whatever meaning's in it.
     I'd better, when I write a villanelle,
     have some cyclical recurrent tale to tell.

Last night I dreamt a poem and I don't mean
I woke with a dream and turned it to words,
but a dream poem, before me on a screen,
with short lines in long stanzas, with each first
line set winking in a colourful marquee.
I scrolled through, sure it was my greatest work.
     The dreamwright had taken elaborate care
     to catch my attention, to shake me aware.

Though I scanned it hard I didn't memorise,
the layout of it had me so beguiled
I have no notion what the meaning was.
I've dreamt poems before – one a racing guide
and another laid out in a straggly maze.
Each time the same, the content slipped my mind.
     That's three entrancing Kubla Khan's I've lost.
     The fault is mine, not anyone from Porlock's.

A childhood outing made 'entrancing' my
artistic yardstick, I want art to enthral,
like a greasepaint and tinsel pantomime:
a poem that will make you jump and call:
'Look out the villain's creeping up behind!'
The Dame turns to us, speaks through the fourth wall,
         but we don't even blink, believe it all,
         then return into a sadly threadbare world.

Now it's me who's threadbare, stiffly factual,
while you make mysterious and troubling lines
in which the world's alive and magical.
And still the luscious clusters of the vine
crush wine into the mouth of coy Marvell,
and the curious peach and nectarine
         themselves reach to him from their grafted tree.
         Not from the world, mundanity's from me.

Letter Five – At the forge

One Monday night, during jazz with Jim McLeod,
a slow elation gathers in my chest.
No joke, but suddenly I laugh out loud.
A bass guitar steps out with impious zest,
I crash to joyful in a single bound.
My waking self's a turtle's carapace,
>   insensible, but art or dreaming harbour
>   a virtue which can penetrate this armour.

Not long after that, I'd not seen you for years,
I was someone different, my marriage gone,
I had begun, perhaps, a union career.
I found your number somehow and I phoned.
I talked Buddhism and thought that I could hear
your hesitation when I got to Zen.
>   Union work took over, Zen was set aside,
>   but remained my base to understand 'inspired'.

My wilful hope that poems might strike sparks,
like the satori slap that jolts you awake,
is from Zen masters – who say the world restarts,
is new, although it is in no way changed.
Their poems are exclamations where they mark
the thunderclap which their enlightening makes.
>   But also, there's a koan in your lightning:
>   in that blue strike-through of all your writing.

The forge is cold, the iron dull, says Char,
his imagination's devastated.
He's writing underground. Throughout his war
his smithy fire is dark, remains forsaken.
In killing, treachery, disgust, nightmare,
he snatches fragments, holding them for later.
      Then, post-war, he reignites the ashes,
      and with his hammer beats out *Leaves of Hypnos*.

I don't claim my life was anything like his,
I fought no wars, declared or clandestine,
but I did a job, for over forty years,
which dried the sap from out my lefty veins.
No spark, my work was all sublunar prose,
a losing fight against repeated wrongs,
      and now I come, at last, to set life down
      that prosy exposition's all I've known.

Letter Six – On being dispensable

It's not long ago that my seventy-fourth
seemed it might define a decent span,
but now I've reached it that's not half enough,
I grow more avid, multiplying plans
to sail to every corner of the earth –
if ever we're released from Covid bans –

>to pale blue headlands fading out of sight,
>to folded ridges blurred by misted light.

I come back in from our one hour of walk –
it's as fine as the springs you'll remember,
when you would meet your girl on the Baillieu lawns
enticed by her and the Melbourne weather;
but my joy in our walk serves to reinforce
how Melbourne and Armidale are severed.

>We check for sweats or sudden loss of taste
>whilst you live in a wholesome paradise.

I'm chained inside and I feel like Ol' Blue,
that deceased hunting dog Joan Baez named,
who's at his own funeral, but listening too,
as they lower him down with links of chain –
they're hollerin' ol' blue, you good dog you,
and how they'll never see his like again.

>I'd no reason to think it my time to go
>but it seems to be expected of me now.

You have to feel their shame for them, they won't
feel it for themselves – not a flinch of shame,
with a flip brusqueness they tell us what's what,
it is what it is and China's to blame,
they foretell our departure within our earshot –
you'll go soon, might as well be now, they're saying:
>I'm sure they're good men and make a good case
>but they've succumbed to a sudden lack of taste.

I don't say they're wrong. I don't wish others,
including my children, shut out of life,
like Le Guin's nameless child in *Omelas,*
who was degraded so others could thrive.
I don't want others condemned to darkness
to vouchsafe me a longer lease on light.
>Oh lord, don't make me be like Abraham:
>who you condemned to sacrifice his son.

It's said wolves do this without palaver,
there's no pretending that it's for your good,
there's no wolfish health economic lather,
they don't dismiss you with a pistol and port,
nor claim it's for the good of all the others.
You're weary, you're toothless and slow of foot,
>it's matter of fact, not being unkind,
>drop by the track, and they leave you behind.

Letter Seven – On the power of memory

I'm ambushed by the *Songs of the Auvergne*
which you played in Carlton way back, when
we shared that place on Newry near the tram.
I say that Proust, though it's central to his plan,
downplays the power of memory's return.
He does not tell how the sinews are unbound,
> how the body buckles with a muffled woe,
> how, covertly, it's conquered, overthrown.

It's now this stilted stanza holds me back –
no way this rigid rinky-dink conveys,
or, better than 'conveys', no way 'enacts',
the hints of recall, then the rush of dense
emotional connection, somehow packed
into a song, no, packed into one phrase:
> Shepherdess, across a gorge, sings to and fro
> *Lèro, lèro, lèro, Baïlèro lô!*

She's with her flock on her side of the stream,
from fifty years ago I hear her call.
Proust does a meditation on his madeleine,
three times descends into his puzzled soul.
Wallace Stevens has a method of his own:
'Three times the thrice concentred self' takes hold –
> now my turn to concentrate has come,
> all of a world is compact in her song.

Our world – the frail asthmatics down the street
from our dingy terrace where I was first
bowled over by the *Judy Blue Eyes* suite
and tried to pick the Mississippi Delta blues.
I watched the moonwalk at Monash then dropped out,
and got casual work on the circular saws;
        then got a steady job, took the tram to town,
        and found I was a gun at Swedish One.

That's not it, is it? That's a half-rhymed list.
Lamely I lament, 'You had to be there.'
There's nothing there depicts how I'm transfixed,
by Canteloube's plaintive Auvergnat air;
how I was moved by the sounds of Swedishness
when I got from Copenhagen to Malmö –
        as a man who's forgotten where he's from
        might quake on hearing sudden noise of home.

You were there, no, not on the Malmö docks,
but when Vin Buckley declared my tuning wrong.
It was, that D-string was always slacking off.
You got us a gig and arranged our songs,
you judged John Fowles by his final paragraph,
and also played those *Songs of the Auvergne*.
        We looked for the house when you were down this year,
        but the terrace row seemed shrunk. We were not sure.

Try again – as Oswald's river nymph would say –
re-merse in these thin waters – try again:
I'm bidding up one sombre autumn day,
I'm heading west like Donne, 1613,
around College Crescent cold-bent in the grey,
walking towards Good Friday in the wind.

       Meagre sunlight chills the General Cemetery.
       The acid wind of years sweeps it away.

'Though these things, as I ride, be from mine eye,'
says Donne, of the Crucifixion in his East,
'They're present yet unto my memory.'
I had almost hoped that Carlton in our years,
if recollected in tranquillity,
could be presented, bodied, in this verse.

       But I'm nowhere near attained to tranquil,
       futile fury hammers at my anvil.

Letter Eight – On politics and art

I'm in no dive on 52nd Street,
it's a Richmond apartment, with a view,
where clouds stack up like clouds that Stevens wrote;
but the last decade was dishonest, low;
and after suffering this pandemic start
how badly can this current decade go?
>I watched the first presidential debate
>and rot with despair. This decade is base.

Best turn to think of politics and art:
how Pissarro's lifelong anarchism ran
through all of him, not abstract, not apart,
but grown into the deepest weave of him,
how his vision of humane common pursuit
is embedded in this apple-picking scene –
>not utopian, they bend and pick and lift,
>while autumn lights them in a golden sift.

Here's a rapid sketch of workers on a wharf
who shovel coal and then heave sacks on board,
and a gouache of peasant girls who bend and push,
like pole vaulters, long pea sticks in the ground;
and Melbourne's busy *Boulevard Montmartre*
puts us right above and central to the crowd:
>There's no need for a moral to be drawn,
>the warmth of solidarity's built in.

Cross the lake from Keswick to climb Cat Bells,
a surge of reverence, of awe, takes hold
when you reach the summit and survey the fells.
A crushing force has creased the land in folds,
settling Derwentwater deep among its hills.
Fells are grazed, ferries ply, humans claim control,
      and yet, subverting our concocted realm
      is the brute, unruly, underpinning world.

That's Wordsworth country, though he turned aside
from the revolution and his girl in France,
was tamed, respectable and sanctified,
already in *The Prelude* he'd unleashed
a bolt which out-burned his urge to moralise,
his counterstrike against rapaciousness.
      We've made him poet of clouds and daffodils,
      but there's disruptive vigour in him still.

Auden would give Cézanne's apples away
for one small Goya or a Daumier.
I suspect the hunt for a rhyme betrayed
Wystan Hugh to this contrarian display.
Cézanne was anti-Dreyfusard to my dismay,
but Pissarro befriended him. Come what may
      there's power in any Cézanne *nature morte*
      to combat capital's defiling force.

Letter Nine – Pandemic, all over the place

One distant vacation you worked a ward
for infectious disease, which now they've closed
(at a vivid second-hand I recall
a younger woman who MS laid low).
Trustingly we allowed you in the door
each night you came home in your working clothes.
    God protect you if you tried that on this year –
    you'd be both paragon and pariah.

The geriatric ward I worked in once
merges with yours in one long airy space:
no monitors, no beeps – just sputum mugs,
patients recumbent spaced in strict arrays.
Those long-off days I was, for once, some use,
sterilising bedpans at the autoclave,
    but now I fade behind the double-glaze,
    set aside and purposeless, disengaged.

How do you write pandemic once removed –
when you don't catch it, or anyone you know?
I didn't rove the squares or ICUs
like the fictional first person in Defoe,
or the doctor in the novel by Camus.
I looked out at the silent street below.
    They directed the aged, we must stay in
    not try good deeds like mad Samaritans.

Bob Dylan wrote it, made it like a sneer –
'You just did what you're supposed to do.'
That's what the Accuser hisses at my ear –
'Self-protective sook! Gutless! You eschew
the appalling actual, outrage, despair,
avoid the stricken, for fear they'll sully you!'
        I washed my hands, obsessive, but it seems
        it's my fastidious nose that I kept clean.

We are finishing Year One of our plague –
heading for Christmas with infections low,
although in fabled Avalon they rage
and Brazil and France, from Maine to Mexico.
Down here we're seven weeks without a case,
and want to secede, as in Boccaccio,
        whose storytellers set a prudent distance
        between themselves and plague in Florence.

I own an urge to blame – the attendees
at protests; premiers, or defiant youth;
runners brushing past, panting out disease;
unmasked angry men, sure Covid is the flu,
the well-heeled back from Aspen with their skis;
bicyclists on foot paths, careering through.
        Masked, I glare with what little face is left –
        they're too busy living to believe in death.

Elsewhere the Lamb's unclasped the Seventh Seal
but we think still to evade disaster's lash.
Invisible, forgotten, scarcely real,
we're the last outpost havoc's yet to reach –
we know the gasping planet's gone to hell,
while we live our variant of *On the Beach* –

      where we await the latest foreign strain
      then beg foreigners to flog us their vaccine.

In a fit of hope I booked for Mudgee,
to ride electric bikes among the vines,
then maybe take the chance to head your way,
to place these letters in your hand from mine.
But the border's closed again, and I could be
ensnared remote from home in quarantine.

      My journey, as infections mount again,
      like these letters, may wander without end.

Postlogue

You say reading Virgil causes drowsiness –
for me it's reading Ashbery's *Flow Chart* –
I doze with it from one page to the next,
half-dreaming my own characters and plots,
who gain themselves a human liveliness,
beyond the scope of word-dependent art.
>   Your fireside may not see much talking done,
>   instead, like Homer, we may nod and yawn.

Time to knock this thing definitively out.
I cast about for one conclusive blow –
there's a wind-torn band of clouds in the south,
fleeing east like pilferers or stragglers thrown
from a battle ground, in perilous rout.
The horizon's a bright duplicitous glow.
>   The traffic rattle fades, the credits roll.
>   My last *ottava rima* is resolved.

In my country

We do not believe in the good faith of the conqueror.[4]

Lockdown morning, thinking of empire[5]

Only two and half of these brilliant days
in any Melbourne June, and these strollers
strike it lucky, who should be pulling beers,
expressing coffee, stacking shelves, or ringing tills –
but they are forced to kick their footloose heels,
sun-ambling, at loose ends, for their own good.

Birds go berserk, tall skies incite their shout.
A whirl of grating calls falls from the hoop pine,
wrenched here as one of transportation's freaks.
Sight of their like, airy pyramids on offshore isles
at New Caledonia convinced James Cook
the place was fortified and these were watch towers.
Then he saw the people in their 'little Stragling Villages'
who were helpful in the finding of fresh water,
('no people could behave with more civility').

Still, he took possession of New Caledonia
as he already took possession of this land –
even longer-occupied, watched-over, cared-for,
a land not for the claiming but itself the claimant,
an old land anciently binding peoples to it,
which gave James Cook not a moment's pause

because he was a very Adam in New Eden –
it was all there for his seizing and his naming,
an innocent fruit dropped in his blameless grasp,
put in reach by mighty Providence and the Admiralty,
and the South Seas kept offering up new lands
in the likeness of the northern coasts he knew,
as proof they'd been waiting for him all along.

Here in the unlikely sun sits Cook's mother's cottage,
brought here brick by brick, by a people grateful
for being discovered, brought here, like these gardens,
piece by piece, their exotic fabric smothering
parched grass, scattered lanky gums and meagre shade,
with green obliteration.

Lessons on water

'Don't think of falling in' – our coach
calls out a spell to ward off ill –
for in the ancient Yarra run
invisible insecticides,
and wild E. coli multiply
despite the poisons, and the pills;
rumours of corpses, draggled rats,
crushed bottles, lurid burger packs,
mush cartons drifting sandwich wrap,
loveliest urban witches' brew.

Throw in a glass of chilled white wine
this could be paradise enough –
two fellow students at the oars
pull stronger every stroke, you feel
a little surge each time they catch
the water with their outstretched blades
and boat slicks over rippled glass,
to where the great trees on the bank
reprieve the river from the blaze
and we slide into easy shade.

No time to let our minds drift off,
soon, in the bow, we'll have our turn
but now our sisters in the stern
(our common effort joins us in
a river-borne sorority)
still haul their oars in unison
while we two figure if they gain
more practice at the work than us –
we watch their bobbing earnest backs,
and envy them their chance to shine.

In this long narrow boat one thought,
one mislaid glance, wrong way, wrong time,
could weigh enough to topple us,
and now we're told what not to think
that's what precisely fills our mind.
A water taxi hurling past
shocks bow-waves out to jostle us –
'Don't think of falling in' we think,
steady the boat with feathered blades,
and think – don't think, don't think, don't think

From the veranda at Shane's vineyard at Everton

Stranded – our ship is blazing to the water line,
flares down beyond the distant line of hills.

Crickets crank their high continuous below the grass
and remnant gumtrees watch beyond the vines.

From across the hill, softly blaring from our right,
comes the bellowing of cattle, an uncouth forlorn.

On a raft of cloud, stone towers and whitewashed walls,
great trees skirting it, an Umbrian hill town glides.

Successive veils of sombre draw across the sky,
cloud-strips darken with a backlit fringe of flame,

and everything comes swimming through a light-filled haze,
comes from its distance, arrives immediate and direct

to where we watch from the valley's eastern lip,
stranded, but conquered also and completely bound;

bound to guess at how it was before our ships arrived,
how it would be to feel this land is yours.

Flight from Yass

Back in the car, too early, in a predawn haze;
sodium lamps make orange of my hands.
Sleep couldn't find my third bed in four days,

plus, there's the wakeful of an aimless man,
with no more purpose than a homing pigeon boasts –
Homeward! Direct me to my distant land.

What an almighty jest – the Holy Ghost
flutters downwards as a strutter after crumbs,
pompous scavenger in dapper morning clothes.

I turn sleepy onto Main Street, west, and some
cowboy, like there's no limit here on speed,
comes high-beam hassling me to Kingdom Come.

On the freeway he skitters past, recedes
to two reproachful dots and then blinks dead.
And leaves the world to darkness and to me.

In their single files reflectors run ahead,
gaze bright-eyed back at me with deep concern,
flick out of sight when I am in most need –

as Aztecs begged their Gods to rise the sun
I pray my road continue out of sight,
not dodge away from how I've guessed it turns.

Though I head west as fast as swallows' flight
soon I'll be gathered by fleet-fingered dawn,
but for now, there's no slight slackening of night.

Through a headlight-carved crevasse I hurtle on,
its overhanging walls occluding stars;
so close I could punch out at airy stone.

Slowly comes, not dawn, but a dull sparse
dim, like the dusk my dead departed to.
No light from air, it comes from things, tall grass

in silent clumps releases gentle glow;
tree trunks and branches cast dull pewter shine,
distinct against the hillsides' indigo.

Hard in the mirror ferocious dazzle blinds,
gold infuses the naked dome of sky,
the blazing wings of dawn beat hard behind
in the rises and the steeps round Gundagai.

Southern Highlands

Pheasants Nest Bridge – Nepean River

By happy accident, deep woven in the web of things,
gravity, topography and concrete make bluff engineers
shape an over-springing elegance, seventy metres up

above the riverbed – from which you glimpse carved
slabs of rock, and treetops in the gorge's daytime dusk,
as you flash across the canyon. You have time to think:

>of your child in Sydney where you cart this load,
>the chipped piano and boxes of their mother's books,
>for whom it's never freeway but slogging through;

>how even this rough bush has been possessed, renamed,
>and whose land this really is – but let one pheasant in,
>next there's gamekeepers with tweedy gentlemen in tow;

>of people living on these gorges, of rock shelters
>beneath the overhangs, and the smoke of your fire
>like a misted skein of meaning on water still below.

Bundanoon Creek

From the topmost brink of the dogleg groove it's gouged,
no sight or distant sound of water; plaited threads
between pools in the rugged gullet of the gorge.

Once this cliff was submarine; sediment was laid
and each next layer pressed the last to sandstone,
and each next layer pressed that last to sandstone.

Then, under-stage hydraulics slid and heaved
and flat stone plains were bared, green gusts
of ocean pouring from them; and then growth:

rivulets hurling cream stone buckshot downstream,
exposed rock weathering to reptilian grey,
open forest advancing steeply from below –

chink! chink! you hear the sound the lyrebird calls,
down in the shade, raking at the dim leaf mould,
chink! chink! the marvellous bird's own voice

when not uttering chainsaws, tractors, whips;
chink! chink! in late summer, long before, or since,
his misty spring of randy fan display and mate and nest.

With a pad and pen

The cliff you look from has its likeness opposite, but cleft –
a jagged V – where a rainstorm waterfall would sluice;
high ridges rule a boundary behind these lower bluffs.

Against the white sky to that north, in silhouette,
are the ridge trees which you trace as curling line,
the pen a seismographic needle linked to eye;

as hand trails, right to left, a knotted script unfurls,
a scripture length of scroll, declared by the power
which says how rock is shaped and trees are held:

> before and beyond you, these were here, this silence
> drifting on bright water; swift sounds of small creatures;
> you are here an instant but the people here before you…

chink! chink! – the land cries out through its local singer,
a stiletto-call dropped point-first in still water,
chink! chink! – which heals without a scar or ripple.

Downstream

Bundanoon Creek pushes down into the Shoalhaven,
which further east bends widely about Bundanon
where Boyd smoothed the river onto copper plates,

his slicked brush catching ragged eucalyptus stands
down the worn escarpment, flood-hurled tree trunks streaked
high and dry, and boulders smoothed to semi-precious;

the sky's an impossible cobalt, the river molten bronze;
there's shadowed clefts like entrance to another world,
but what other world could there be than this river, cliffs?

After Uluru

This sovereignty is a spiritual notion: the ancestral tie between the land, or 'mother nature', and the Aboriginal and Torres Strait Islander peoples. – *Uluru Statement from the Heart*[6]

I believe the balance sheet of Australian history is a very generous and benign one. I believe that, like any other nation, we have black marks upon our history but amongst the nations of the world we have a remarkably positive history. – Prime Minister John Howard[7]

How is theft and conquest 'generous and benign'?
No incidental blemish but calamity in our foundation.
A generous people would confess – all we have is built
on acts which would be wrong if they were done to us.

If Howard came and took my home, my livelihood,
my paint and canvas, my wok and my guitar,
then reviled me as I starved outside his door,
I would carp, go on a bit, knotted with grievance.
I'd plot my reinstatement and revenge, and aim
to force on him the dispossession he inflicted;
and he, victor, would live with the prickling sensation
that someone, somewhere, wishes him profoundly ill.

But…having sovereignty for sixty thousand years,
having seen the continent and its islands seized,
its rivers, lakes, mountains, marshes, straits,
parcelled out to strangers, then ruined, razed,
and having been cast out, hunted from the lands,
its peoples now propose to share with us,
whose only claim to right was that we had the guns,
their continuing sovereignty which 'shines through'
but not so as to displace our usurping Crown.

That treasure that we could not take by force,
the spiritual sovereignty in the land from ages,
is within our reach – if we could raise ourselve
to respond with fair play and clear-sightedness;
could value that ancestral tie aright and treat
with the first comers, the custodians, as equals.
Then without presumption, we or our children,
might join those who tend the land forever,
become undivided patriots, say we belong.

Translating Bonnefoy's snow in desert

Yves Bonnefoy goes to teach in Williamstown, MA.
From the Loire, he's landed in the land of the Big Snow;
I translate his snowy poems, as I travel inland
where there is no word for snow, that I have heard.

I should know snow – I was there at Boston's founding,
two student weeks shut up in Winthrop's journals:
the murder of a chief who was told he had safe conduct,
the killing and enslavement of the Pequot people.

You see why I think of Boston at Australia's centre?
Cattle stations broader than small nations, stolen,
cultures, spirits, custodians for millennia,
set at naught by men righteous with guns and Christ.

Bonnefoy counts snowflakes in the ones and twos
and blizzards; descending his back steps he views
a white field like a snowy page inscribed
with an infinite amaze of chipmunk tracks.

Here, there's unyielding sky and rock face,
shadow-incised by morning on the slant,
like scars from when the canyon came of age.
To try deciphering them would be a trespass.

For Bonnefoy, sometimes, summer falters, sunders,
reveals an utter frigid at the base of being;
for me, there's this hard secret at the centre:
in the land I belong to I'm as alien as snow.

In my country

In my country there are people who were always here
and those who were not but have nowhere else.

In my country you hear thanks from the nowhere-else
to those who washed up here looking for somewhere else,
and that the German King of England took the land,
and brought British civilisation to the always-here.
60,000 years of stewardship seems like no time at all
to the nowhere-else people, who have been here
a tick over two hundred, which is time immemorial.

Many with nowhere else will yell ferocious – here is ours!
They own the land. They fought and died for it. Often.
Ours by conquest only, although we have nowhere else.
I ran in yellow fields and sailed from yellow beaches
and the people they belonged to, the people always here,
were bundled out of sight and mind as if they never were.

The township where I grew was run by nowhere people,
who yearned to return to an elsewhere verdant 'Home';
a township run by men in tweed who told us to be proud
of a foggy homeland, an Empire of grateful swarthy peoples,
enraged if it were to be said we are beneficiaries of theft.

In my country our nowhere-else leaders give thanks:
that we are moderate, sensible people, who do not seethe
with the uncouth ethnic passions which divide other lands;
that there was no notion of race superiority in our founding;
that in our foundation is benevolence for less blessed peoples;
that we never knew the terrors of war on our soil,
save a couple of comic opera rebellions by Irish criminals,
the bombing of Darwin and the shelling of Sydney.
Dispossession, at gunpoint, of the always-here people,
does not count. We pretend we made our paradise from scratch.
Because here, we say, were a scattered few in vastness,
who did not know the wealth of what they roamed.

In my country you will hear them say 'get over it',
'toughen up' or 'that was long ago', 'move on'.
This is the way of history – some conquer, others
are conquered and the losers should be gracious.

In my country – I don't say my country.

Notes

1. Vivaldi Concerto in C (for diverse instruments) RV558
2. Theodore Roethke, *Words for the Wind*, Indiana University Press, 1965
3. A film directed by Ingmar Bergman, 1957
4. René Char, 'Partage Formel VII' (translation by David Bunn), *Fureur et mystère*, Gallimard, 2010
5. René Char, 'Qu'il vive', 1950 (translation by David Bunn)

May it come to pass

This country is no more than a wish, an anti-tomb

In my country the tender signs of spring and badly clothed
    bird are preferred to distant goals.
Truth awaits dawn beside a candle. Window glass is
    neglected. What does it matter to the watcher.
In my country we don't ask questions of a person who is upset.
No shadow of evil falls on a capsized boat.
A half-hearted greeting is unknown in my country.
We only borrow what we can return improved.
There are leaves, many leaves on the trees of my country. The
    branches are free not to have fruit.
We do not believe in the good faith of the conqueror.
In my country we say thanks.

6. Sarah Holland-Batt in her note to her poem 'Last Goodbyes in Havana' refers to Raymond Carver's 'Morning, thinking of empire'
7. Uluru Statement from the Heart – https://ulurustatement. org/the-statement
8. John Howard, weekly Hansard, 30 October 1996, cited by Dr Mark McKenna, 'Different Perspectives on Black Armband History', 10 November 1997, http://aph.gov.au/ About_Parliament/Parliamentary_Departments/Parliamentary _Library/pubs/rp/RP9798/98RP05

Previous publication

'White gull' was published in the *Australian Poetry Anthology 2015*.

'Elantxobe' was published in the *Global Poetry Anthology* from the Montreal International Poetry Prize 2015 and an earlier version of 'Atocha 2004' was published in the *2011 Global Poetry Anthology*; both anthologies are published by Véhicule Press under the Signal Editions imprint.

A longer version of 'In dreams let us not use first names' was joint winner of the Gwen Harwood Prize in 2012 and was published in *Island* magazine issue 131.

'Lavender' was published in the anthology *Long Glances* drawn from entries to the 2013 Jean Cecily Drake-Brockman Poetry Prize under the auspices of Manning Clark House.

Earlier versions of some poems appeared during 2010 on David Bunn's blog 700 Homely Verses. Those poems include 'Grevillea'.

About the author

David Bunn is a Melbourne writer who worked for many years in Australian trade unions. His first book of poems *The Great Scheme* was published by Ginninderra Press in 2021. The poems in this volume are drawn from his published and unpublished writing over the last decade and include responses to the Uluru Statement from the Heart and to what social media asserts was the longest lockdown in the world. His website is *One moment human* (davidbunnpoetry.com).